Marilyn Dillon

Don't Wrestle, Just Nestle

Jesus Is Victor

Don't Wrestle, Just Nestle

CORRIE TEN BOOM

Fleming H. Revell Company
Old Tappan, New Jersey

Unless otherwise identified, Scripture quotations are from The Living Bible, Copyright © 1971 by Tyndale House Publishers, Wheaton, Illinois 60187. All rights reserved.

Scripture references identified PHILLIPS are from THE NEW TESTAMENT IN MODERN ENGLISH (Revised Edition), translated by J. B. Phillips. © J. B. Phillips, 1958, 1960, 1972. Used by permission of Macmillan Publishing Co., Inc.

Scripture quotations identified KJV are from the King James Version of the Bible.

Poem by Annie Johnson Flint is used by permission. Evangelical Publishers, Toronto, Canada.

Library of Congress Cataloging in Publication Data

Ten Boom, Corrie.
    Don't wrestle, just nestle.

    (Her Jesus is victor)
    1.   Christian life—1960–   I.   Title.
II. Series.
BV4501.2.T38   248'.4   78-14214
ISBN 0-8007-0848-2

Contents

Foreword

"Baby, just cry. Don't look at the people or mind what they are thinking about you. Just cry." I felt an arm around me, hid my face on her shoulder, and cried. Then I heard her singing softly:

> His eye is on the sparrow,
> And I know He watches me.

Yes, my comforter was Ethel Waters. I had heard her sing those words before, but they had never touched me so. For this time, she was singing that song for me, and I needed her song.

This happened the first time I saw the movie, *The Hiding Place.* In my mind I found myself reliving the suffering of my family. I saw Father and Betsie, both lost in prison. I had to put up with the horrible cruelties again. That was why I cried.

But then my eyes were turned in the right direction by Ethel Waters' song. There *is* One who watches me, and the secret of abundant life is literally "Don't wrestle, just nestle." What a security!

1

Prescription for Anxiety

Why should I feel discouraged, Why should
    the shadows come,
Why should my heart be lonely And long for
    Heav'n and home,
When Jesus is my portion? My constant Friend
    is He:
His eye is on the sparrow, And I know He
    watches me.

"Let not your heart be troubled," His tender
    word I hear,
And resting on His goodness, I lose my doubts
    and fear;
Tho' by the path He leadeth But one step I
    may see:
His eye is on the sparrow, and I know He
    watches me.

Whenever I am tempted, Whenever clouds arise,
When songs give place to sighing, When hope
    within me dies,
I draw the closer to Him, From care He sets me free;
His eye is on the sparrow, and I know He
    cares for me.

MRS. C. D. MARTIN

This century has been called the Age of Anxiety. How fitting that description is! Everywhere I go, I find people tormented by inner tensions, nervous strain, worries, and fears. We are a generation of worriers, always taking pills to cure our anxieties and relax our nerves.

There is a great deal of difference between worry and concern, and we must realize this. Concern makes us do something to ease the situation. It moves us to take constructive action. But worry burdens our minds and bodies without helping us to find a solution to the problem. Worry is like racing the engine of an automobile without letting in the clutch. You burn energy, but you don't go anywhere.

No doctor has a cure for worry. Oh, he can give you an aspirin for your headache or something for your nervous stomach. He may even give you one pill for your tensions and another pill for your insomnia. But these are not cures. They just cover up the real problem.

There is a permanent cure for worry. The prescription is not mine—it was given by Jesus almost two thousand years ago, in His Sermon on the Mount. He devoted a great deal of this talk to the problem of anxiety. Therefore, here is His prescription for anxiety.

Remember the Power of God

A few weeks before the Sermon on the Mount, Jesus walked along the shore of the Sea of Galilee and called twelve men to lay down their fishing nets and follow Him. They would be His disciples. The men saw the presence of God in Jesus. They wanted to follow Him, but still, they had questions—many questions.

"If we don't fish for a living, how will we support our families?"

"How can we be fishers of men? We're afraid to talk to other people."

"How can we carry the Gospel to the world? Just the thought of doing that fills us with fear!"

Jesus went up on a mountain to escape the huge crowd that kept following Him. When He was in a private place, He sat down, gathering His disciples around Him. He began to teach them about the Kingdom of God. The disciples, who had followed Jesus for a little while now, knew He had no money of His own. Yet He never worried. He seemed content.

"What is the secret of happiness?" they asked.

Jesus replied:

. . . don't worry about living—wondering what you are going to eat or drink, or what you are going to wear. Surely life is more important than food, and the body more important than the clothes you wear. Look at the birds in the sky. They never sow nor reap nor store away in barns, and yet your Heavenly Father feeds them. Aren't you much more valuable to him than they are? Can any of you, however much he worries, make himself even a few inches taller? And why do you worry about clothes? Consider how the wild flowers grow. They neither work nor weave, but I tell you that even Solomon in all his glory was not arrayed like one of these! Now if God so clothes the flowers of the field, which are alive today and burnt in the stove tomorrow, is he not much more likely to clothe you, you "little-faiths?" So don't worry and don't keep saying, "What shall we eat, what shall

we drink or what shall we wear?" That is what
pagans are always looking for; your Heavenly
Father knows that you need them all. Set your
heart first on his kingdom and his goodness, and
all these things will come to you as a matter of
course. Don't worry at all then about tomorrow.
Tomorrow can worry about itself! One day's trouble is enough for one day.

Matthew 6:25–34 PHILLIPS

Actually, Jesus was chiding them a bit, saying "You
already have life and a body, and they are far more
important than what to eat and wear. Does it not follow
that the God who is capable of making a human body
is capable of putting clothes on it and providing food
to keep it going?"

The next time you find yourself depressed or worried about some big problem, remember the power of
God. Remember His great miracle of bringing you into
being, and you will know He is more than able to care
for you.

I remember reading a story about Bishop Quayle,
who must have had a keen sense of humor. He told of a
time when he sat up late in his study, worrying over
many things. Finally the Lord came to him and said,
"Quayle, you go to bed. *I'll* sit up the rest of the
night."

A friend of mine told me, "When I worry, I go to the
mirror and say to myself, 'This tremendous thing that
worries me is beyond solution. It is even too hard for
God to handle.' And then I smile."

Remember the Foolishness of Worry

Jesus had a way of asking embarrassing questions.
"Which of you by taking thought can add one inch to

your height?" Can you worry yourself taller? Or
shorter? You might worry yourself dead, but never will
you worry yourself happier. That comes by a different
method.

Alcoholics Anonymous has sound advice to offer
their people—advice all of us could use—in the
prayer, "O God, give us serenity to accept what cannot
be changed, courage to change what should be
changed, and wisdom to distinguish the one from the
other."

I like that, for there are two things we should not
worry about: the things we can change (we need to get
busy and do something about these) and the things we
cannot change (no amount of worry will help these).
Instead, we should let God give us the courage and
strength to master the unavoidable, for with God,
nothing is impossible.

"Don't be fools; be wise: make the most of every
opportunity you have for doing good. Don't act
thoughtlessly, but try to find out and do whatever the
Lord wants you to do" (Ephesians 5:16, 17).

Jesus says that God is concerned about us personally. "Look at the birds of the air," Jesus said to His
disciples. "God feeds them in spite of the fact they
cannot drive a tractor, plough a field, or work a harvest-
ing machine. They can't even build barns to store the
grain. Yet God takes care of each one of them." Then
He turned to His disciples, and I imagine He had a
slight smile on His face. "Are you not of more value
than they?"

Next Jesus pointed to the wild flowers that were
poking their heads around the rocks in the hard soil of
Israel. "Look at them," He said. "They can't run a
spindle or loom, they don't even have the ability to sit

down at a sewing machine and make their own clothes. But see how beautifully God has dressed them. Why? Because God cares for even the grass of the field." Then He said, "If God so clothes the grass of the field, will He not much more clothe you?" (*See* Matthew 6:25–30.)

Count Your Blessings

I was in Japan, very tired, with a stomach that was upset from the unusual food. How I longed for a good European meal, a table where I would not have to sit crosslegged on the floor, and a soft bed instead of the hard mats the Japanese sleep on. I was filled with self-pity. I wanted to be back in Holland!

That night in church, while I was busy feeling sorry for myself, I saw a man in a wheelchair. After the service my interpreter took me down to meet the man, a bent little fellow with yellow skin and slender hands. His face wore the happiest expression I could imagine.

"What are those little packets on your lap?" I asked the man, pointing to several packages wrapped in brown paper and tied with string.

He broke into a wide grin and tenderly unwrapped one of the packages. It was a sheath of pages covered with Braille, the raised script of the blind. "This is the Gospel of John, written in Braille. I have just finished it," he said.

Then he continued. "This is the fifteenth time I have written the Gospel of John in Braille. I have also written other of the Gospels, as well as many shorter portions of the Bible."

"How did you come to do this?"

"Do you know about the Bible women here in Japan?" he asked. "Bible women go from village to village, bringing copies of the Bible, books, and literature to those who are hungry for God. Our Bible woman is very ill with tuberculosis, but she travels every week to sixteen villages, even though she will soon die. When I heard about it, I asked the Lord what I could do to help her.

"Although my legs are paralyzed, and I cannot get out of the wheelchair, in many ways I am healthier than she. God showed me that though her hands are shaky and my legs paralyzed, I could be the hands, and she the legs. I punch out the pages of Braille, and she takes the Bibles around to the villages and gives them to the blind people, who miss so much because they cannot see."

I left the church that night filled not with self-pity, but with shame. Here was I, with two good legs for traveling all over the world, two good lungs, and two good eyes, complaining because I didn't like the food!

These precious people had discovered a sure cure for self-pity—service to others. Perhaps it is like the slogan I once saw on a church sign in America. "If you are unhappy with your lot in life, build a service station on it." The best antidote I know for self-pity is to help someone else who is worse off than you.

"I complained that I had no shoes, then I saw a man who had no legs, and I stopped complaining."

Walk With God

Does the Lord Jesus say, "Come along now. Take it easy. Don't worry," leaving us to realize that there have never been so many reasons to worry as there are now?

No! The Lord gives an answer.

"Seek first his kingdom and his righteousness" (*see* Matthew 6:33 KJV). It is your relationship with your heavenly Father that is important. That is what determines whether you will be victorious or defeated, however difficult the circumstances are.

The day after He fed the 5,000, Jesus chastised the crowd that followed Him, accusing them of following Him because He had fed them. "But you shouldn't be so concerned about perishable things like food. No, spend your energy seeking the eternal life that I, the Messiah, can give you. For God the Father has sent me for this very purpose" (John 6:27).

Still the crowd was more concerned with food. They asked Him to give them free bread every day, as Moses did in the desert. Jesus told them, "Moses didn't give it to them. My Father did. And now he offers you true Bread from heaven. The true Bread is a Person—the one sent by God from heaven, and he gives life to the world" (John 6:32, 33).

The crowd, still not understanding what Jesus was telling them, asked that they might have every day the bread He was describing.

"I am the Bread of Life. No one coming to me will ever be hungry again. Those believing in me will never thirst," Jesus told them (John 6:35). Although He said this over and over again to the crowd, they still failed to understand or accept. Many of His disciples left Him at this point. Jesus then turned and asked the twelve if they, too, were leaving Him.

Simon Peter answered for all of them: "Master, to whom shall we go? You alone have the words that give eternal life, and we believe them and know you are the holy Son of God" (John 6:68, 69). Peter and the others who stayed with Jesus knew what was important and what was not. They knew the way to victory.

With your hand in the Father's hand, you stand on victory ground. Give room for the Holy Spirit. He gives you the right outlook on troubling events. I know that from the time that I saw my sister Betsie starving in a prison camp. We were surrounded by people who had behind them a training in cruelties, but we had moments when we were conscious that we were walking with the Lord.

Often we had to go too early to roll call, which started at 3:30 A.M. Betsie and I would walk through the camp, and there were three of us present. Betsie said something, I said something, and the Lord said something. I can't tell you how, but both Betsie and I understood clearly what He said. These walks were a bit of heaven in the midst of hell. Everything around us was black and dark, but in us there was a light that belonged to eternity.

Jesus said:

All who listen to my instructions and follow them are wise, like a man who builds his house on solid rock. Though the rain comes in torrents, and the floods rise and the storm winds beat against his house, it won't collapse, for it is built on rock.

Matthew 7:24, 25

From My Notebook

Today is yesterday's tomorrow you worried about, and all is well.

If God sends us on stony paths, He provides strong shoes.

Faith is blind—except upward. It is blind to impossibilities, and deaf to doubt. It listens only to God and sees only His power and acts accordingly.

S. D. GORDON

Jesus is always victorious. We only have to get into the right relationship with Him and we shall see His power being demonstrated in our hearts and lives and service. And His victorious life will fill us and overflow through us to others. That is revival in its essence.

ROY HESSION

Worry is the interest you pay on trouble before it comes.

God will not tolerate anything in our life that takes the supreme place which is His by right.

Jesus Christ can transform our . . .

> fear into faith
> anxiety into adoration
> worry into worship.

2

No Time for Anxiety

. . . Our fears for today, our worries about tomorrow, or where we are—high above the sky, or in the deepest ocean—nothing will ever be able to separate us from the love of God demonstrated by our Lord Jesus Christ when he died for us.

Romans 8:38, 39

We were in Africa. Prisoners were dancing. The pounding rhythm created an atmosphere of demonical darkness. The expressions of the dancers' faces made me afraid. It was as though they were dancing themselves into a trance, possessed by dark powers. Their shouting influenced the other dancers, causing the gloomy darkness in their eyes to increase every minute.

These people were criminals. They knew what it was to be inspired by hell itself. Next to me were three black Christian brothers, who had accompanied me to this place hidden far away in the jungle—the place where I was to speak. We waited for the prison director to join us.

At last he came. He was a friendly man, but I could see that he knew how to make people obey. "I am so

19

glad you came to speak to my men." He clapped his
hands and shouted, "Stop dancing! Sit down and listen
to what Miss ten Boom has to tell you."

I saw the anger flash in their eyes. It was hard for
these men to part from the spirits who had kept them
in their power. About four hundred men settled down
in front of me, and about two hundred were standing
behind me. I saw not one friendly face among the six
hundred: I looked at my three black Christian brothers
and felt uneasy that not one white man had accompanied me. I underestimated those men badly, as I
later clearly discovered.

I softly prayed, "Lord, I know that those who are
with me are more and stronger than those who are
against me. Let your never-failing love fill my heart
and mouth, and also the man who will interpret for
me."

I spoke rather a long time to those prisoners, and I
saw the expressions on their faces change as they
heard me say, "Jesus loved *you* when He died on the
cross for the sins of the whole world." I never saw
such a dramatic change in people. They came from
darkness into light; from the darkness of hell into the
light of heaven.

As we waited at the gate while a guard found the
key, a prisoner came running toward me. He took my
hand and said something. My interpreter translated,
"You came to us because God's love is in you. Thank
you. Thank Him!"

We squeezed into the tiny car and headed down the
primitive path through the jungle, going toward Kampala. The moment we got into the car, my three
brothers began to sing and praise the Lord. I was sitting in the front seat, squeezed against the driver. The

other two men were crowded into the tiny back seat.
But even our cramped positions did not keep them
from singing and praising God as we roared through
the dense jungle.

What a strange sight we must have been, bouncing
down the jungle road, weaving from side to side to
miss the holes and puddles, singing and praising the
Lord in loud voices!

I saw a man ahead, standing on the side of the nar-
row road. He had the tire and wheel from a car leaning
against his leg. The driver slowed the car to a stop and
shouted across me, "What is the matter, my friend?"

"Please bring me to Kampala," he pleaded. "My tire
is flat, and my wheel is broken."

What a pity we have no room, I thought.

But my happy black brothers saw no such problem.
"Of course," they shouted together. "Join us. We like
to help our brothers in the name of Jesus."

The man came around to the other side of the car, to
get into the front seat between the driver and me.
While he was walking around, one of the men in the
back seat leaned forward and whispered. "Pray with
us, Tante Corrie, that we bring him to the Lord before
we reach Kampala."

How they squeezed him in, I'll never know. But
soon we were on our way again, the man jammed between the driver and me holding that big, rusty car
wheel and the dirty black tire on his lap. The men in
the car began singing and praising the Lord again,
keeping time with the bumps in the road.

The driver began to talk to the man in his own language, and the other men enthusiastically entered in. I
could not understand what they were saying, but I
knew they were talking to him about the Lord Jesus. I

prayed, keeping my eyes on the road.

Suddenly the passenger looked at the driver and said something. One of the men in the back seat interpreted for me. The passenger was asking if he knew the driver. Hadn't they met before?

"Sure," the driver answered. "Last year you and I were in the same prison, where we have just been with Miss ten Boom. You know, boy, at that time I served the devil. Now I serve Jesus Christ. He uses me to save lives of other sinners, and He will use you from now on, also."

The man with the big wheel on his lap listened intently. Before long, he accepted Jesus as his Saviour. I wanted to join in the men's happy praises, but I was too concerned about the road and the wild way in which the driver was swerving from side to side. *Surely we'll all be killed.* I worried.

Then, ahead, we saw a woman with two children waiting alongside the road. "Let us give her a lift and also bring her to Jesus," one of the men shouted.

Did he really mean it? There was absolutely no room!

The car stopped, and for a minute I entertained the hope that they were just going to witness to her where she was and drive on. But no, they motioned her to join us in the car!

As she got in the back seat with her two children, I saw a third child come out from under her coat. Somehow they all got in, sitting on top of one another. One of the small children had to crawl over my shoulder and sit on my lap. I could not feel my legs. Never, never had I been in such an overcrowded automobile—and on such a terrible road.

We started up again, the car rolling from right to left,

left to right, bouncing off rocks and logs alongside the road, weaving over shaky jungle bridges. But the black men were tremendously happy, believing the Lord had put the woman there so they could pick her up and witness to her. This time, all four of the men—including the one with the big wheel on his lap—eagerly joined in the conversation, telling the woman about the Lord Jesus Christ.

Suddenly the four men began to sing. *"Tuku tenderesa Jesu,"* an African song of praise. The woman had accepted Jesus as her Saviour and Lord.

We arrived in Kampala and swerved through the traffic, the men still singing and banging their hands against the side of the automobile in time with the music. Our fellow travelers left us—the man with the big wheel and the woman with her three children—but not until my friends had obtained their names so they could follow up their work. Then they took me to the place I was staying.

After they had gone, I sat for a long time, rubbing life back into my legs and trying to get some insight into the events of the afternoon. While I, the cautious European, had been so anxious and worried about the fierce prison, the horrible road, the old car, and the discomforts and dangers of the trip, my black brothers had no time for anxiety. They were too busy praising God and sharing the good news with those whom God sent into their path. They did not see the people along the road as problems, but as opportunities.

Perhaps, I thought, as I lay back on the bed to rest my aching body, if I would spend less time worrying whether the car would run, the road was paved, or the bridges would hold—and lose myself in praise and service as these African brothers did—I would not only live longer, but more abundantly. While I was anxious about reaching my destination, they were excited about meeting people along the way. Reaching the destination seemed almost incidental to praising God and serving Him as they went.

Maybe the way in which we travel and the attitude we have while making our way through life is more important than reaching our destination. Or could it be that, in God's sight, the way actually *is* the destination?

Jesus said ". . . I am the Way—yes, and the Truth and the Life . . ." (John 14:6).

From My Notebook

It is better to burn out than to smolder out without having warmed one heart for the Lord Jesus.

Happiness is not dependent on happenings, but on the relationship that persists in the happening.

When we act on the Word of God, and not on our feelings, we experience that God means His promises. The fact is that God watches over His Word to perform it.

> Slow me down, Lord,
> I am going too fast,
> I can't see my brother,
> When he is going past.
>
> I miss a lot of good things
> Day by day,
> I can't see a blessing
> When it comes my way.

When the heart has learned to trust Him as He should be trusted, utterly without reservations, then the Lord throws wide the doors of the treasure-house of grace. He bids us go in with boldness and receive our share of the inheritance of the saints.

Be sure you remain covered with a canopy of praise. It is like a tent over and around you. Satan has no entrance as long as you pin down the sides by praising, and thank God for His wonderful promises.

In the life of the true believer there are no accidents.

My little children, I am telling you this so that you will stay away from sin. But if you sin, there is someone to plead for you before the Father. His name is Jesus Christ . . . .

1 John 2:1

3

Worry

Don't worry over anything whatever; whenever
you pray tell God every detail of your needs in
thankful prayer, and the peace of God, which sur-
passes human understanding, will keep constant
guard over your hearts and minds as they rest in
Christ Jesus.

Philippians 4:6 PHILLIPS

Before the battle, the general always sends his spies
into the enemy camp. They take photographs of secret
defenses, they learn the enemy's battle positions, their
ammunition supply points, even the personal weak-
nesses of the opposing leaders. But unless the general
passes this information on to his own troops, they cannot win the battle.

That is why I want to share with you some of the
things I have learned about the enemy and about the
Victor, Jesus Christ. I want you to know that God expects us to be conquerors over the powers of
darkness—not only for the sake of our personal victory
and for the liberation of others who are in bondage to
Satan, but for His glory. He wants the world to know
that He is triumphant and victorious, and the only way
it will ever know is by our demonstration of God's
power and authority.

Once a man saved up his money for years and bought the house of his dreams. It was in the countryside, with mountains and streams all around it. He could not wait to begin living in his new house, but because of his business, he could not move in for several months. So he allowed the man who was living there to stay as a caretaker until he was ready to move in himself.

But when the new owner came to move into his dream house, the other man said, "No, I am staying here. You find somewhere else to live."

"But you promised you would move out when I was ready," the owner said.

The man gave a laugh and replied, "This is my home. You cannot come in." Then he slammed the door in the owner's face and locked it.

The owner marched straight to the police station with his papers of ownership. The next time he knocked on the door of his house, there were two large policemen standing next to him. When the man in the house saw the policemen, he meekly packed his belongings and left the house to its owner.

What the true owner of the house could not do in his own strength, he was able to do when he appeared with authority on his side. It is the same with us. Satan may laugh at us and continue to afflict us with disease, fear, anxiety, and defeat. But when we come to him in the name of Jesus, he knows we have all the authority of the Kingdom of God behind us, and he must flee.

Worry Is Sin

I had to learn that worry is sin before I could get rid of the worry. First I tried to "fear not" as an act of obedience. It was as successful as trying to kill a lion with a toy gun. Then I began to learn the secrets. First you must ask forgiveness for your sin of worry. Then you need to accept the cleansing of the blood of Jesus. Finally, you need to let God fill you with the Holy Spirit. When you are filled with the Holy Spirit, the spirit of fear will flee, forced out by power and love and a sound mind.

In the latter part of 1946, a group of Christian ladies in Ottawa asked me to give my testimony at an evening meeting.

I did not even know where I would sleep that night, but I went in obedience. I felt it was a training in trusting God. How good that the coach was the Lord Himself!

It was the first time that I had been in Canada. I remember that the spirit of worry was very busy with me. Sometimes my traveling went smoothly. God gave me friends who organized my meetings, and I went where He told me to go. But now I was not quite sure of the Lord's guidance. At such moments I felt far from Holland. A big ocean was between my hometown and me.

So often that tramp for the Lord, the prisoner Paul, had helped me. I opened my Bible and read what he wrote from his prison in Rome: "Be careful for nothing; but in every thing by prayer and supplication with thanksgiving let your requests be made known unto God. And the peace of God, which passeth all understanding, shall keep your hearts and minds through Christ Jesus" (Philippians 4:6, 7 KJV).

My, but Paul knew about worry! Still, he found the answer: "I can do all things through Christ which strengtheneth me" (Philippians 4:13 KJV).

I did not even know where I would sleep that night, but God had used Paul to encourage me, and I trusted Him.

That evening, I told my problem to the dear people who heard my talk, and sure enough, a lady came to me and said, "You are very welcome in my home. I have a small guest room you may use." I had been worried about finding a place to sleep, but the Lord had the answer all worked out for me!

What a joy to be surrounded by kind people. Before I fell asleep, I thought of the time shortly before, when enemies were all around me, and how they hated me because of what I had done for the Jews. Soon I was sound asleep.

Suddenly the light in my room came on. I opened my eyes, and a uniformed officer was standing in front of me. My only thought was, *This is the Gestapo. They have found me.* I said to the man, "I am not a Jew." Then I remembered where I was and told him that I was a guest of the lady of the house. Without a word, the man put the light out and left.

What had happened? He was the owner of the house and had come home late. He did not want his wife to see him at that hour, especially since he had been drinking too much that night. He decided to go to the guest room, but his plan misfired because of my presence there. When he told his wife, she was very disturbed. What a shock it must have been for her guest! She put on her robe and ran to my room. There she found me, fast asleep!

Some months later, I met my host again. It was a bitterly cold evening. I had spoken that afternoon in a town some distance from Ottawa, where I was to speak in the evening. Friends had brought me to a house halfway between the two towns, and my former host was waiting there. He told me that he was going to take me to Ottawa, where the meeting was to start at 8 P.M.

The highway was so icy that we skidded from right to left. I looked at my friend and saw that he had given himself courage for the drive by taking some drinks, and it was not a little amount that he had enjoyed. I thought about the coming evening. How could I sit for hours in that car, worrying about the slippery road and his driving, and then still have the power to speak? I couldn't. I was worried—I thought I had reason to be—but I knew that my worry was a sin. I would have to ask forgiveness for my sin and trust the Lord to deliver us safely to Ottawa.

I prayed for strength and then said to the driver, "Jim, I am going to speak tonight, and it is impossible for me to worry for several hours beforehand, while you skid from right to left and left to right. So I hope you don't mind, but I am going to sleep."

Jim smiled and said, "You go ahead. I will drive and not sleep." And he did. The Lord gave me a very good rest.

The young girl who was my secretary at that time was sitting behind me, and she told me later that I snored all the way. That was a comfort to her, because she knew that I was not worried, but she said it was still the most terrible car ride of her life. We arrived safely, on time for the evening meeting, and I was refreshed and ready for my talk.

God's Armor

The battle always has to be fought before the victory is won, though many people think they must have the victory *before* the battle. The conflict with worry and fear is almost always there—each person must overcome or be overcome. But we must fight each battle of our lives in the strength of Jesus' victory. He said, "As the Father has sent me, even so I am sending you" (John 20:21). We are to be like Jesus—One of whom Satan is afraid!

When we worry, we are carrying tomorrow's load with today's strength; carrying two days in one. We are moving into tomorrow ahead of time. There is just one day in the calendar of action—today. The Holy Spirit does not give a clear blueprint of our whole lives, but only of the moments, one by one.

We all have the same enemies—we are all preyed upon by frustration and worry. In India, Australia, Japan, Germany—we need the same Holy Spirit. We need to remember that we are children of God, living within His constant care. God knows and is interested both in the hardest problems we face and the tiniest details that concern us. He knows how to put everything in place, like a jigsaw puzzle, to make a beautiful picture.

But Satan has a very good secret service. The moment you step out from under God's umbrella of grace, you are discovered and attacked by Satan. Recognition of Satan's attack is half the fight. An attacking enemy who is not recognized already has half his battle won. Never knowing where, how, and when Satan will attack us, we should never be unprotected or unprepared. We need to be clothed with the whole armor of God.

Last of all I want to remind you that your strength must come from the Lord's mighty power within you. Put on all of God's armor so that you will be able to stand safe against all strategies and tricks of Satan. So use every piece of God's armor to resist the enemy whenever he attacks, and when it is all over, you will still be standing up.

Ephesians 6:10, 11, 13

What a relief to know that we do not need to provide the armor! God makes the armor—we just put it on. But the armor has no protection for the back, for God does not expect any deserters. Neither is the armor a museum piece—it is given for use on the battlefield. Jesus is Victor!

Every temptation to worry or fear is an opportunity for victory. It is a signal to fly the flag of our Victor. It is the chance to make the tempter know anew that he is defeated.

Thine, O Lord, is the greatness, and the power, and the glory, and the victory, and the majesty: for all that is in the heaven and in the earth is thine; thine is the kingdom, O Lord, and thou art exalted as head above all. Both riches and honour come of thee, and thou reignest over all; and in thine hand is power and might; and in thine hand it is to make great, and to give strength unto all.

1 Chronicles 29:11, 12 KJV

From My Notebook

Worry is a cycle of inefficient thoughts, whirling around a center of fear.

Worry is often carrying a load that one should not carry at all.

Worry is distress of mind, not concern. Some people ought to have *more* concern.

It is sinking under the sense of responsibility, yielding to the fear that there may be failure, instead of gripping the lines and whip and determining to ride down the chance of its coming.

S. D. GORDON

God gives us His power to bear all the sorrow of His making. But He does not give us the power to bear the sorrows of our own making, which the anticipation of sorrow most assuredly is.

IAN MACLAREN

The purpose of being guilty is to bring us to Jesus. Once we are there, then its purpose is finished. If we continue to make ourselves guilty—to blame ourselves—then that is sin in itself.

4

May a Christian Worry?

Why, therefore should we do ourselves this wrong,
Or others—that we are not always strong,
That we are ever overborne with care,
That we should ever weak and heartless be,
Anxious or troubled, when with us is prayer,
And joy and strength and courage are with Thee.

AUTHOR UNKNOWN

We imagine that a little anxiety and worry are indications of how wise we are. We think we see the dangers of life clearly. In reality, however, our fears are only an indication of how wicked we really are.

As Charles G. Trumbull says:

Worry is sin; a black, murderous, God-defying, Christ-rejecting sin; worry about anything, at any time whatever. We will never know victory over worry and anxiety until we begin to treat it as sin. For such it is. It is a deep-seated distrust of the Father, who assures us again and again that even the falling sparrow is in His tender care.

The words *fear not* occur many times in the Bible. The word of God has no suggestions; only commandments. So if we fear and worry, we are being disobedient, and disobedience is always a sin.

The only way blunders and destruction can occur in our lives is when we forget to trust God. When we take things into our own unskilled hands, we get everything knotted and tangled.

Worry is utterly useless. It never serves a good purpose. It brings no good results. One cannot think or see clearly when worrying. Let pagans worry, if they will, but we must not, for we have a living Saviour, our Lord Jesus Christ, and His conquering power. His victory can be our victory. Life at best is brief, and there is so much to be accomplished. If we must burn ourselves out, let us burn out for God.

In this age of increasing pace, it is so easy to follow the crowd and let materialism become, our god. But if we do, only too often we find that worry and tension become our masters. The effects of tension are seen in all spheres of life. Tension leads to inefficiency and frayed nerves with our fellow workers and students. In politics, it leads to strain in international relations and fears of war. In the home, tension leads to irritability with our husband or wife, destroying the very thing God meant to be perfect.

For with people who are not content, worry has a fair chance. Paul writes:

". . . I have learned to be content, whatever the circumstances may be. I know now how to live when things are difficult and I know how to live when things are prosperous. In general and in particular I have learned the secret . . . of facing either plenty or poverty. I am ready for anything through the strength of the One who lives within me" (Philippians 4:11–13 PHILLIPS).

Lonely Contentment

I have never been so poor as the time that I was in solitary confinement. How difficult it was to learn to be content. But Paul wrote once, while in prison, that we are God's workmanship. I experienced the same. The lessons were difficult, but the Teacher was so powerful. The Lord was my all-sufficiency. I wrote home: "The Lord Jesus is everything to me. He never leaves me alone. I concentrate on the Saviour. With Him there is certainty, with the other things, only uncertainty and delayed hope, which hurts the heart. Once I asked to be freed, but the Lord said, 'My grace is sufficient for you.'"

That brought my thoughts to Paul. *He* had to learn a lesson. Three times he asked the Lord to take away the thorn in the flesh (*see* 2 Corinthians 12:8). Then he got this answer: God's grace was sufficient for him. That was true for Paul and it was true for me. In a way I knew that there was a danger that the joy I felt and my security in Him would lose some of their power when I was free; when the securities of the world would once again be a comfortable foundation to rest upon.

When the Lord gives you the ability, through His grace, to accept the situation, that contentment can help you to get rid of your worry, whatever happens. But could I ever accept being a prisoner alone in a cell? I surely could not, but Paul told about all grace, always, in all things (*see* 2 Corinthians 9:8).

Once when I was in the cell, I heard the bolt on the outside of my door being undone. A guard opened the door and commanded, "Follow me!" I was being called out to be questioned. It was the first time I had left the cell during that lonely imprisonment. Yes, lonely—night and day I was alone. First we had to go through long corridors with cell doors on both sides, then through a door which opened onto the outside. I breathed deeply. I was in a courtyard. The walk was almost too short to the small barracks where people were questioned. I looked up to the sky, then around me, and then down and saw blades of grass and some tiny white flowers. The little flower "Shepherd's purse" was growing between the bricks used to pave the courtyard.

When the guard who accompanied me looked the other way, I quickly bent down and picked some of those little flowers and hid them inside my dress. When back in my cell, I took a broken medicine bottle, arranged my bouquet, and put it behind my cup so that the guards could not see it when they looked through the peephole in my door. That tiny bouquet was my garden, and I enjoyed it as the only nice thing in my cell.

I was ready to accept my little bouquet of six blades of grass and three little flowers as my garden because of Him who was in me, and I could say then with Paul, ". . . I look upon everything as loss compared with the overwhelming gain of knowing Christ Jesus my Lord. For his sake I did in fact suffer the loss of everything, but I considered it mere garbage compared with being able to win Christ" (Philippians 3:8 PHILLIPS).

Demon Influence

When we are worrying, we are not trusting. Yet we who have burdens and responsibilities are inclined to worry. Again, it is so important that we recognize the enemy. Worry and depression are sister and brother. I want to tell you about something that I experienced—a time when the influence of depression was practically nationwide.

After I was released from the German concentration camp, I returned to Holland until the war was over. Then God told me to go back to Germany, to carry the good news of Christ's victory over fear and guilt. When I arrived in Germany, however, I found the people in great confusion. Many German people had beloved relatives missing. Were they still in Russian concentration camps? Had they died in battle or in the horrible bombings? This uncertainty drove many people to desperation.

Many of these people were turning to the fortune-tellers to find their answers. While the evil spirits, working through the fortune tellers, often gave just enough accurate information to keep the people coming back, something else also happened. Many of those who visited the fortune tellers later developed horrible fears, depression, and anxiety. Their hearts, it seemed, were always in the gloom of darkness. They often had the urge to commit suicide. I immediately recognized this as sure evidence of demon influence.

Jesus said, "I am the Light of the world. So if you follow me, you won't be stumbling through the darkness, for living light will flood your path" (John 8:12). Even if a child of God has visited a fortune teller and come under demon influence, he does not have to remain in darkness. He can be set free.

Realizing this, I began speaking against the sins of the occult. It was the occult that was putting people in bondage, causing them to break down mentally and spiritually. I often read Deuteronomy 18:10–13 to point out how these sins are an abomination in the sight of God. Instead of depending on God's power, the people were rushing to the enemy for help. And as we know, the enemy is a liar, whose very purpose is to deceive people and lead them away from the truth.

I showed the German Christians how Jesus Christ has provided an answer to this serious problem. Satan is not the Victor, Jesus is. And even if the people had invited the demons in, Christ could overcome that. They did not have to live with their depression or fear any more. They had to be set free. I was able to say to them:

> . . . [God] gave you a share in the very life of Christ, for he forgave all your sins, and blotted out the charges proved against you, the list of his commandments which you had not obeyed. He took this list of sins and destroyed it by nailing it to Christ's cross. In this way God took away Satan's power to accuse you of sin, and God openly displayed to the whole world Christ's triumph at the cross where your sins were all taken away.
>
> Colossians 2:13–15

In the Old Testament there is an interesting story of the lost axhead. A son of the prophets had been chopping wood, and his axhead had fallen into the Jordan River. Since it was a borrowed ax, he was worried and afraid. He ran to Elisha for help. Elisha sent him back to the place where he had made his mistake, so the miracle of restoration could happen. The axhead floated to the surface, the young man grabbed it and replaced it on the handle (*see* 2 Kings 6:1–6).

Just so, you need to go back to the place where you opened the door of your life to the influence of the spirit of worry. Where did the fear enter? What was it that caused you to start worrying? Remember, the spirit of fear does not come from God. Instead, God gives us power and love and a sound mind (*see* 2 Timothy 1:7). Therefore, you need to ask the Lord Jesus to close the door that you opened.

How is this done? First you need to recognize that you have sinned. Most fear, anxiety, and worry come through the sin of not trusting God.

Second, confession is necessary. Face yourself. Tell God. And then, if possible, confess to someone close to you. When all of this is done, you may then claim the precious promises for cleansing. You will instantly be freed from the bondage of Satan.

Worry is a demon—fear of demons comes from demons themselves. As children of God, we have nothing to fear. He who is with us is much stronger than he who is against us. "And he asked them, 'Why were you so fearful? Don't you even yet have confidence in me?' " (Mark 4:40.)

"The seed among the thorns represents those who listen and believe God's words but whose faith afterwards is choked out by worry and riches and the responsibilities and pleasures of life . . ." (Luke 8:14).

May we worry? We have a whole Bible as our guide, Jesus Christ as our living Saviour who loves us, and heaven as our future!

From My Notebook

Worry is an old man with bended head,
Carrying a load of feathers which he thinks are lead.

Worry means two enemies—the thing you worry about and the worry!

Why don't we try something lighter than worry? Worrying people are like tightrope walkers going over a rope from the past to the future. They balance between hope and fear. In one hand they carry a sack with the undigested past, in the other hand a sack with the anticipated future.

The heart lays aside its fears amid the accumulated blessings of our heavenly Father. Worries pass away like cloudlets in the warmth of a summer's morning.

> Yesterday He helped me,
> Today He did the same.
> How long will this continue?
> Forever, praise His name.

42

5

Fear

For God hath not given us the spirit of fear; but of
power, and of love, and of a sound mind.

2 Timothy 1:7 KJV

Fear is the atmosphere of worry. Nothing weakens
us as much as fear. On the other hand, nothing
weakens the tempter as much as a quiet, bold, steady
fearlessness. Satan cannot operate in the atmosphere
of trust.

Oh, but fear and worry can talk so wisely! You may
often think they are right, but fear is often a stupid
blunder. Once I worked for a month in Los Angeles
during a flu epidemic. One morning my secretary
woke up with a bad headache, and I feared that she
had the flu.

"Girl, please stay in bed. I have to go to a college to
speak at nine o'clock, but I will go alone," I told her.
Once I was outside, I felt a headache myself. My eyes
felt so strange. I knew that headaches and eye problems were sometimes symptoms of the flu, and I worried all the way to the college. I had so much work to
do—I didn't have time for the flu!

Once at the college, I opened my Bible to begin my
talk and found that I could not read even one letter!
Fear whispered, "You have the flu in your eyes." I was

not sure that was possible, but I listened to my fear. What would I do if I could not read? I need to prepare for my talks and to study the Bible, if I am to speak about the Lord. Could I go back to my former trade of watchmaking? Impossible! I would need my eyes more for that than for any other trade.

I know that I did not give a happy talk that morning, for when worry and fear are on the throne, you are not an open channel for streams of living water. It is impossible to listen to the Lord's voice while listening to your own fear. Fear is so loud, so insistent, so time-consuming!

Near the end of my talk, my secretary came quietly into the room and sat down in the back row of the auditorium. When I finished my talk and the students left, I went to her. "Why didn't you stay in bed, when you had such a headache?"

"Oh, I am not ill. My headache is gone," she answered.

"All right, but it could have been the beginning of the flu. You should have stayed home and started answering the letters that I gave you."

"That's why I came. I couldn't work, because you have *my* glasses!" Both our glasses had exactly the same frame, but far different lenses! We both laughed at our mistake. My flu had gone. So had my headache. Once we traded glasses, I could read perfectly, and I was ashamed to have listened to my silly, blundering fear all morning.

Trust the Vine

Anxiety, fear, and worry are the result of our unwillingness to trust God. To worry is the same as saying to God, "I don't believe you." Do you fear for your finances? Are you afraid you won't be able to feed or shelter your loved ones? Do you lie awake and fear your fears? Listen to what God says!

"Give your burdens to the Lord. He will carry them. He will not permit the godly to slip or fall" (Psalms 55:22).

"And it is he [God] who will supply all your needs from his riches in glory, because of what Christ Jesus has done for us" (Philippians 4:19).

"Stay away from the love of money; be satisfied with what you have. For God has said, 'I will never, *never* fail you nor forsake you.' That is why we can say without any doubt or fear, 'The Lord is my Helper and I am not afraid of anything that mere man can do to me'" (Hebrews 13:5, 6).

Remember when Jesus told the parable of the vine and the branches in John 15? He said the secret to abundant living is in staying attached to the vine. An unattached branch has something to fear. Not only can it not produce fruit, but it will be burned in the fire. But an attached branch has no fears. All it has to do is nestle close to the vine, and the vine does all the work, sending its sap through the branch and producing luscious grapes. It is not the branch that produces the grapes, it is the vine.

"But if you stay in me and obey my commands, you may ask any request you like, and it will be granted! My true disciples produce bountiful harvests. This brings great glory to my Father" (John 15:7, 8).

Fear does not take away the grief of yesterday, nor does it solve the problems of tomorrow. All it does is rob you of the power of today. Rather than wind up on a psychiatrist's couch or an undertaker's slab, do what

God tells you. Seek first His Kingdom and His righteousness. He will add everything else you need.

Fear or Victory?

There are many people who don't realize that fear is the enemy. When the fight is on and blows are being exchanged, fear is a sure element of defeat. Fear sucks the spirit out of one's fighting, takes the nerve out of one's courage, robs vim and zest from one's action. But this is always a false fear, because it tells us the enemy is stronger than we are. That is not true! We know that Jesus is Victor, and a fear that tells us otherwise is false.

When you become a child of God, you are a target for the enemy, and he will do his utmost to tell you that you are crazy. Sometimes you think that you are not a Christian when you have trouble, but I should very much doubt whether you are a Christian at all if you did *not* have trouble.

The whole of the New Testament and the history of the Church shows that when we are children of God, we are in a fight of faith. Not having any troubles in your life is therefore far from being a good sign. It is indeed a serious sign that there is something radically wrong. There is a special reason for my saying that, because we are special objects of the attention of the enemy. Why not have problems when it is God's way to bless you!

". . . count it all joy when ye fall into divers temptations" (James 1:2 KJV). That is the way your faith is proved. The devil cannot rob us of our salvation, thank God! But he can make us miserable. He can fill us with his false fear.

It is the tempter who knows real fear. His fear is

founded on fact and experience. He has met One greater and stronger than himself. Satan is afraid of his Victor. He knows what it means to be thwarted and resisted, beaten back steadily and driven clear off the battleground. There has been a man upon the earth whom Satan fears—whom he can neither trust nor resist—Jesus Christ. He learned to fear Him in Nazareth and in the wilderness. Jesus' absolute, steady obedience to the Father beat Satan. Even the storm on Galilee's blue waters, so unusually violent that it frightened the experienced sailors, failed to touch Jesus with fear.

Fear is as common as sin. If we could be wholly free of fear, we would have stronger bodies, minds, spirits, faith, courage, and power. The tempter continually plays on our sense of fear. For instance, people's fear of being in personal want is holding back huge amounts of money—money which could change the condition of the whole heathen world and move forward the date of Jesus' coming.

At our side there is always conflict with the tempter. Each of us must overcome or be overcome. Our victory comes through Jesus' victory, and we must fight in the strength of His victory. Throw out your self-seeking spirit—it allows Satan a free hand to do as he chooses. Yield to the Holy Spirit. He will burn out your self-spirit.

Men as Trees Walking

In his book *Spiritual Depression, Its Causes and Cure,* Dr. D. Martyn Lloyd-Jones wrote about the great importance of living as rich as we are in Jesus Christ.

If all Christians simply began to function as the New Testament would have us do, there would be no problem of evangelism. It is because we are failing as Christian people in our daily lives and witness that the Church counts for so little and so few are attracted to God. So for that most urgent reason alone, it behooves us to deal with this question.

We are like the man who was blind and healed, but still saw men as trees walking (*see* Mark 8:22–26). Yes, we have received the healing touch from Jesus—we were born again the moment we asked Him to come into our hearts—but people around us are not envious to receive the same. This is simply because we do not behave like happy, fearless people. We have unlimited riches through the promises of the Bible and the presence of the Lord in our hearts, but we still see men as trees walking.

Jesus asked the blind man, "Can you see?"

The man answered, "Not quite one hundred percent, Lord." How good it was that he told the Lord! Jesus gave him another touch of healing, and his eyesight was perfect. I am sure that even if Jesus had not asked him, the man would have told the Lord the problem and been satisfied.

So, if your sight is still only partial, tell the Lord, "Thank You, Lord, for what You did, for what You gave me—but I need more."

For Jesus said, "Blessed are they which do hunger and thirst after righteousness: for they shall be filled" (Matthew 5:6 KJV). He did not tell the blind man, "Try hard to see." The man had only to ask, and it was given to him.

You and I must ask Jesus to do the job through His Holy Spirit. He is the One who makes our eyes to see.

"But when the Holy Spirit controls our lives he will produce this kind of fruit in us: love, joy, peace, patience, kindness, goodness, faithfulness, gentleness and self-control . . ." (Galatians 5:22, 23).

We are often too content with a partial healing. I had an experience of liberation from resentment some time ago. Some friends, fine Christian people, had done something really mean against me, and I had forgiven them. That is what I thought.

A friend asked me how the situation was, but I told him, "I don't want to talk about it. I have forgiven it."

"I understand that," he answered, "but I should like to know what they think about it."

"Oh, they take it easy. They simply say that they have never done it. Perhaps they forget that I have everything in black and white, in the letters which they wrote to me at that time."

My friend looked at me and waited a moment. Then he said: "Where are *your* sins? You told us in your talk this morning that when we confess our sins, God casts them into the depths of the sea and you even believe that there is a sign saying No Fishing Allowed. But the sins of your friends you have in black and white. 'Lord, I pray that you will give Corrie the grace to burn all the black and white of the sins of others today as a sweet-smelling sacrifice before she goes to bed.' "

I surely did, and how well I slept that night. Now when I meet these people, I enjoy a peace that makes our friendship an unusual joy.

No, it was not easy. As a matter of fact, I needed the Lord just as much as when I had to forgive the people who had been cruel to my family. Forgiving is a hard job. But in 2 Corinthians 9:8 Paul tells us that there is always grace, sufficient for everything. The Holy Spirit taught me a prayer that always helps me, "Thank You, Lord Jesus, that You brought into my heart God's love through the Holy Spirit. Thank You, Father, that Your love in me is stronger than my resentment" (*see* Romans 5:5).

No compromise. The Lord is willing and able to give us clear sight. When worry gets static, it becomes depression. When unforgiveness is healed, there is a liberation that makes the enemy run.

Have you the black and white of the sins of others? Burn them today. Together with the Lord, you can.

Children of the Light

One time, artists were invited to paint a picture of peace. The pictures were many and varied, but the winner depicted a little bird sitting calmly on her nest, which was built on a slender branch overhanging Niagara Falls. The peace of the little bird did not depend on her surroundings. And so it is with us. As Christians, our peace of heart and freedom from fear do not depend on our circumstances, but on our trust in God. Fear is want of faith.

Being a Christian does not mean there is no more battle. It means we have a strategic point of attack in the battle. The battle position of the Christian is victory, joy, and abundance. The Lord expects us to do no more than welcome His assistance. The doors of heaven are open. If I hold on to feelings that prevent me from living under an open heaven, then it is no wonder I am fearful and depressed.

A great note of joy and victory is sounded in the book of Philippians—a book, incidentally, written from prison. Here Paul says:

Don't worry about anything; instead, pray about
everything; tell God your needs and don't forget
to thank him for his answers. If you do this you
will experience God's peace, which is far more
wonderful than the human mind can understand.
His peace will keep your thoughts and your hearts
quiet and at rest as you trust in Christ Jesus.

Philippians 4:6, 7

It is God's intention that we live as children of the
light. He wants us to be strong, free, peaceful, and
happy. This was the secret Nehemiah learned when
he was tempted to come down from the wall he was
building around the city of Jerusalem. On every side
there were worries and fears, but he grasped God's
truth and sang, "The joy of the Lord is my strength"
(*see* Nehemiah 8:10).

Now I have a very practical tip for you. Take good
notice of all the blessings He gives and all those He
has given in your past. As the old hymn says, "Count
your many blessings, count them one by one, and it
will surprise you, what the Lord has done."

> Faith came singing into my room,
> And other guests took flight.
> Grief, anxiety, fear and gloom,
> Sped out into the night.
>
> I wondered that such peace could be,
> But Faith said gently, "Don't you see,
> That they can never live with me?"
>
> **ELIZABETH CHENEY**

From My Notebook

There is an aggressiveness of love that is fearless. Fear is cowardly. Faith is aggressive, like love and goodness are aggressive. Satan is aggresssive in evil, but Jesus is more aggressive in love.

Jesus Christ knows no fear, and He expects you to fear nothing while He is with you. When we confess His lordship and our hearts fully agree, then we turn our lives over into His care. That is the end of worry and fear and the beginning of faith.

Worry is double-parking on the avenue of anxiety.

$$-\text{Christ} = +\text{fear}$$
$$+\text{Christ} = -\text{fear}$$

Courage is fear that has said its prayers.

The folly of being anxious about the near future is just as stupid as worrying about what will happen about a thousand years hence. We have to live in the present moment, because we can do nothing about the past, and God is doing everything about the future.

GEORGE MACDONALD

God has made me put my heel on the neck of worry, of weakness, of fear, of inability, and I stand and declare that whosoever believes in Jesus shall not be put to shame.

E. W. KENYON

6

Frustration

Even if we have learned how to deal with anxiety, worry, and fear, the enemy has yet another powerful weapon he uses on us—frustration. Frustration is dangerous because it is so simple to blame it on others, to think there is nothing *we* can do to overcome the problem. And yet even the most frustrating of circumstances can be turned to good, if we use the opportunities we have.

I find it a great frustration to have a message but have no one to give it to. On one trip to Russia I had such a frustrating time! I wanted to tell everybody, especially the communists, about the Lord Jesus Christ. However, whenever I tried to talk to people on the streets of Moscow, I found they would always be looking over their shoulders. Finally they would rush away, afraid someone would see them talking to the old woman with a Bible. I became so frustrated, anxious, and filled with despair. I was in Russia, but I could find no one who would listen!

One afternoon I met a young woman, and we chatted about ordinary things—the weather, the tulips in Holland, the price of gasoline. I sensed she was hungry to hear more about the Lord, but I knew she was afraid to talk in the park. I invited her to come to my hotel room for a good talk.

"Oh, no," she whispered, glancing every which way. "The tourist hotel rooms here are the most dangerous places to talk. There is a hidden microphone in each room. Every word you speak is put on a tape and played before the officials." She excused herself and moved quickly away from me.

The next morning my companion and I were sitting in our hotel room, totally defeated. We had been in Russia one week and had not been able to speak to a single communist about the Lord Jesus.

Suddenly I spotted something on the floor, just under the edge of the bed. It was a pattern of tiny holes, like those in the top of a pepper shaker. Suddenly I had a tremendous inspiration. "Thank You, Lord," I said to myself. "That surely must be the place where the microphone is hidden." Reaching for my Bible, I bent low over the holes in the floor and began to speak in a deliberate voice.

"You who listen have many problems, just like every other human being. Two of these problems are common to all men—sin and death. I have here in my hand a book. It almost bursts with good news. In this book—it is called a Bible—you can read everything you need to know about the answers to these problems. The answer is found in the life of a man, the Son of God, Jesus Christ. He died on the cross for the sins of the whole world, and for your sins also. He carried the punishment you and I deserve. But not only did He die for us, He rose from the dead and is alive today. Yes, He is even willing to live in you through His Holy Spirit. If you will accept Him, He will give you the power to overcome death also and live forever with God in heaven."

For almost five minutes I preached into the hidden microphone, knowing that my sermon was not only being heard, but was being recorded on a tape recorder and passed on to superiors. What a joy! I finished my sermon by saying, "Jesus said once, 'Come unto me, all you who labor and are heavy laden, and I will give you rest.' Since all men in Russia know the meaning of labor, then it means that Jesus must love Russians in a special way. When He says 'all,' He is talking to all who listen to this tape."

From that day on, I gave the microphone a little sermon every morning, bringing a simple Gospel message and hope to my unseen hearers.

After leaving Moscow, we traveled to Leningrad, where once again I discovered the pepper-shaker holes in the floor. That night I gave a five-minute sermon to my hidden listeners. The next morning, two serious men came in and took a seat at the table next to ours at breakfast. From their appearance and the way they dressed, I was sure they were members of the secret police.

For a moment I was disturbed and frustrated. Then I saw what God was doing. My microphone sermon had brought results! Instead of being worried, I should rejoice. This was simply another opportunity to present the Gospel.

I asked my companion, in English, "Do you know that you can become a child of God?"

She immediately grasped what I was doing and began to play her role. "I can never be a child of God," she said, shaking her head. "I am not good enough."

"Ah ha," I answered. "That is exactly what I expected you to say! But you see, only sinners are eligible." As we talked I kept noticing the two men at the

next table. They tried to pretend they were not interested. One man had a newspaper in front of his face.
But I could see they were leaning in our direction,
trying to hear every word.

We continued our conversation, speaking as loudly
as we could without making it obvious. We stayed at it
until we were satisfied these men could never say they
had not heard the Gospel. We even repeated the
whole conversation in German, in case they couldn't
understand my English!

Do you think I was playing a silly game, talking into
hidden microphones and giving my testimony at
breakfast? It was no game at all! After one whole week
of frustration, I was at last giving my message to the
communists. Not in the way I would have preferred, it
is true. But who can say that those few men who heard
me were not important to the Lord? Even when we are
denied a big opportunity, we must make the best of all
the little ones that come our way.

I remember a story about the little boy and his sister.
They were trying to climb a steep mountain. The little
girl began to complain, "Why did God put all these
rocks here?"

Her brother reached back and patted her on the
shoulder. "These are really stepping stones," he said.
"God put them here to help us reach the top."

Many people are worried and frustrated because
they never have the opportunity to do what they want
to do. I have found the seeming obstacles are really
opportunities within themselves. If we do what our
hand finds to do, then God will open up broader places
of service.

Many years ago I heard of an old Dutchman and his
young son. They had to walk home at night across the

polders, the dried sea bottom where the water had been pumped out and held back by dikes. The little boy was afraid, for he knew there were still deep pockets of water and many patches of quicksand on the polders. All they had to give them light on the walk was a small kerosene lantern.

"Please, father," the boy begged, "don't make me walk out there. It is so dark, and the lamp only gives light enough for one step at a time."

The father took his son's hand in his own. "That's right, but one step at a time is all the light we need. And if we walk in the light we have, we have enough light for the next step. However, if we stand still, waiting for enough light to see the entire way home, then even the light we have will burn out, and we will be left in the dark."

And so they made their way home safely, one step at a time, walking in the light. Every obstacle, every frustration, can become an opportunity if we trust God and walk in the light we have.

From My Notebook

You are on the road to success if you realize that failure is only a detour.

In order to realize the worth of the anchor, we need to feel the stress of the storm.

When a train goes through a tunnel and it gets dark, you don't throw away your ticket and jump off. You sit still and trust the engineer.

Our trust and hope are not in the promises, but in the One who made the promises.

Our faith may falter, but His faithfulness, never!

We are to do heavenly business. The earthly part of it is only a detail.

> Some wish to live within the sound
> Of church and chapel bell
> I want to run a rescue shop
> Within a yard of hell.
>
> C. T. STUDD

We will see more and more that we are chosen not because of our ability but because of His power that will be demonstrated in our not being able.

What can you and I pray for leaders? Pray for the Christian leader that God will guide him. Pray for the non-Christian leader that God will control him.

Faith sees the invisible, believes the unbelievable, and receives the impossible.

Luther said, "Work as though He will not be coming for a thousand years. Be ready as if He should come today."

Men have to go through many experiences in order to get the spiritual vision which is needed to see the divine plan. A film is always developed in a dark room.

7

Don't Burden Yourself

Let him have all your worries and cares, for he is always thinking about you and watching everything that concerns you.

1 Peter 5:7

Many years ago, shortly after World War II had come to a close, I was invited to speak in a Japanese church in Tokyo. The nation was still reeling from the impact of the war. All that the Japanese people had believed in had been snatched away, and two of their greatest cities had been destroyed by the atomic bomb. If ever a people had reason to worry, it was the Japanese.

Because of the language barrier, it seemed practical for me to give them an object lesson. "Do you know the feeling," I began, "when your heart is like a suitcase with a heavy load?"

The sad-faced people in the little church all nodded. They knew the feeling.

I picked up my suitcase and put it on the table. It was very heavy. I told them how weary I was from tramping all over the world, carrying that suitcase filled with heavy objects.

"My heart was like that until just last week, when I

read a glorious verse in the Bible. It says, 'Cast all your anxieties on him, for he cares about you.' I did that. I brought all my burdens to the Lord—all my cares— and I cast them upon Him." I opened my suitcase and spread it out on the table to demonstrate. "Lord," I continued, "here are my co-workers. They are so tired." I reached down and took two items out of the suitcase and laid them on the table.

"And here is my trip, Lord—the one I have to make next week to the town where I don't know a single person. You know how worried I am about that, and how afraid I get when I think about it. I cast this care on You, too, Lord." I took a big package out of the suitcase and laid it on the table next to the two smaller packages.

"Here are my friends at home, Lord. They wrote about a car accident. Will You please heal them?" I took out one more object and placed it on the table.

"And here is that boy who refused to give his life to Jesus. Dear Lord, You know how much I have worried about him." I placed a heavy piece on the table.

"This is my unbelief. Almost always when our hearts are heavy, it is because we have an unconfessed sin. Forgive me, Lord, and cleanse me with Your blood. Holy Spirit, give me faith and trust."

I took object after object out of the suitcase, mentioning each one as a particular burden or worry. "This is my pride. This is my self-seeking . . . ." In the end, the suitcase was empty, and I said, "Amen!" I closed the empty suitcase and pretended to walk out of the room, swinging my light bag as though it were made of paper.

The people immediately got my point, and the light of understanding broke on their faces. I could tell by

their smiles and polite bows when I was finished that
the Holy Spirit had spoken truth to them.

After the meeting I quickly threw all the items back
into the suitcase and dashed off with my host, to go to
the home of the wonderful Japanese Christians who
entertained me until it was time to fly on to Hong
Kong.

Many years passed, and then I found myself in
Berlin, at an international congress on evangelism.
After one of the morning seminars, a distinguished-
looking Japanese evangelist approached me. "Corrie
ten Boom," he said with a broad smile, "every time I
hear your name, I think of your trouble suitcase."

"Oh," I said, flattered, "I am so glad you remembered what I said that night."

"It was not what you said that I remember," he
smiled courteously, "it is what you did."

"You remember me taking all those objects out of my
suitcase and laying them on the table as an illustration
of how to pray?"

"No, that is not what I remember most," he said.
"What I remember most is that after you finished your
talk, you took all the objects, put them back in your
suitcase, and walked out of the hall just as burdened as
when you came in."

Oh, what a vivid object lesson! That afternoon, back
in my hotel room, I began to take a good look at myself.
Was I guilty of doing that in my life? How easy it is to
unpack my trouble suitcase each morning and cast all
my cares on the Father, because He cares for me. But
then, as the day goes on, I keep coming back and pick-
ing up first this care and then that one, slipping them
back into my suitcase. By the end of the day, I am just
as burdened as I was at the beginning, and far more

exhausted, for I have had to keep slipping back to pick up the cares originally given to my Father.

What about you? Did you unpack your trouble suitcase this morning? Good! But what did you do afterwards? Is your heart still as burdened and heavy as it was before you prayed? Did you repack your suitcase as soon as you emptied it? If so, perhaps you need to return to the Lord, casting all your cares upon Him— for He cares for you. Tell it to Him. The Holy Spirit will teach you how to pray and leave your burdens with the Lord.

Live One Day at a Time

When Jesus told His disciples, "Therefore do not be anxious about tomorrow, for tomorrow will be anxious for itself," He was saying, "Don't try to carry today's burden *and* tomorrow's burden at the same time."

One evening a man stepped into the kitchen to help his wife with the dishes. As he was working, he thought, "If that poor woman could just look ahead and see the dishes that remain to be washed in the future, towering like a mountain ahead of her, she would give up right now!" Then he laughed. "But she only has to wash tonight's dishes, and she can handle that."

As you may know, I grew up in a clock shop. My father was a watchmaker, and I was the first woman in Holland to be licensed as a watchmaker. Our home, the Beje, was filled with the sound of ticking clocks. I still remember the old Dutch parable about the clock that had a nervous breakdown.

The little clock had just been finished by the maker, who put it on a shelf in the storeroom. Two older clocks were busy ticking away the noisy seconds next to the young clock.

"Well," said one of the clocks to the newcomer, "so you have started out in life. I am sorry for you. If you'll just think ahead and see how many ticks it takes to tick through one year, you will never make it. It would have been better had the maker never wound you up and set your pendulum swinging."

"Dear me," said the new clock. "I never thought about how many ticks I have to tick in a year."

"Well, you'd better think about it," the old clock said.

So the new clock began to count up the ticks. "Each second requires 2 ticks, which means 120 ticks per minute," he calculated. "That's 7,200 ticks per hour; 172,800 ticks per day; 1,209,600 ticks per week for 52 weeks, which makes a total of 62,899,200 ticks per year. Horrors!" The clock immediately had a nervous breakdown and stopped ticking.

The clock on the other side, who had kept silent during the conversation, now spoke up. "You silly thing! Why do you listen to such words? That old grandfather clock has been unhappy for years. Nobody will buy him, and he just sits around the shop gathering dust. Since he is so unhappy, he tries to make everyone else unhappy, too."

"But," the new clock gasped, "he's right. I've got to tick almost sixty-three million ticks in a year. And they told me I might have to stay on the job for more than one hundred years. Do you know how many ticks that is? That's six billion, two hundred million ticks. I'll never make it!"

"How many ticks do you have to tick at a time?" the wise old clock asked.

"Why, only one, I guess," the new clock answered.

"There, now. That's not so hard, is it? Try it along with me. Tick, tock, tick, tock. See how easy it is? Just one tick at a time."

A light of understanding formed on the face of the clock, and he said, "I believe I can do it. Here I go." He began ticking again.

"One more thing," the wise old clock said. "Don't ever think about the next tick until you have your last tick ticked."

I understand that was seventy-five years ago, and the clock is still ticking perfectly, one tick at a time.

No man sinks under the burden of the day. It is only when yesterday's guilt is added to tomorrow's anxiety that our legs buckle and our backs break. It is delightfully easy to live one day at a time!

From My Notebook

I took a burden to the Lord
To cast and leave it there.
I knelt and told Him of my plight,
And wrestled deep in prayer.

But rising up to go my way
I felt a deep despair,
For as I tried to trudge along,
My burden was still there!

Why didn't you take my burden, Lord?
Oh, won't you take it, please.
Again I asked the Lord for help,
His answering words were these:

My child, I want to help you out
I long to take your load
I want to bear your burdens too
As you walk along life's road.

But this you must remember,
This one thing you must know . . .
I cannot take your burden
Until you *let it go.*

BETTY CURTI

8

Prayer

Then another angel with a golden censer came and stood at the altar; and a great quantity of incense was given to him to mix with the prayers of God's people, to offer upon the golden altar before the throne. And the perfume of the incense mixed with prayers ascended up to God from the altar where the angel had poured them out.

Revelation 8:3, 4

Sometimes we underestimate the value of our prayers. In the book of Revelation, we read how precious they are in God's eyes. They are so precious that they are all preserved there.

When I read this text, I understand a little bit of the great value that our prayers have in the eyes of the heavenly Father. Look back on the prayers you have prayed for that person you are worrying about. Not one of those prayers is lost. They are kept in heaven. What a comfort. What an encouragement!

When Do God's Answers Come?

The Bible says that by prayer and supplication with thanksgiving we should let our requests be made

67

known unto God. Have you ever been discouraged about your praying? Does it seem your prayers are never answered? Much of our anxiety comes as we worry about others. This isn't helped, it seems, if we pray for others and then do not see our prayers answered. However, let me tell you a few stories that I think will give you encouragement to go on, despite seeming failure.

Not very long ago, I had a wonderful experience in my home country of Holland. I was invited to appear on national television, to bring the Easter message. More than six million people heard my message, I was told. But the most wonderful result was hearing from some people I had not heard from in years—people I had prayed for many years ago.

One man wrote to me and said, "Twenty-five years ago I came out of a concentration camp, into the house you opened for ex-prisoners. You brought me the Gospel. I thought I was not ready for it, but you told me you were going to keep on praying, anyway. Last night I saw you on TV, and now I can say with all my heart, 'I have accepted the Lord.' " It took twenty-five years, but God answered my prayer for that man's salvation!

Another man telephoned. "Forty-five years ago, you told me exactly the same thing you said tonight on TV—that Jesus was the Son of God and is still alive. I always refused to accept Jesus as my personal Saviour. Now I am ready to say yes to Him. May I come to see you?"

Of course I replied, "Please come."

We talked and prayed together. "Now," I said, "ask Jesus to come into your heart."

He prayed, "Jesus, I cannot open my heart. Please, won't You force the door?" And Jesus did a miracle in the life of that man—an answer to my prayer after forty-five years.

When I was fifteen years of age, I spent some time at a secular domestic-science school. Most of the teachers and students did not want me to talk about the Lord. Therefore I spent time praying for them. Following the TV broadcast, I received a letter saying, "Sixty years ago we were together at the domestic-science school. I suddenly remembered that you often talked about the Lord Jesus when we were together. I saw and heard you on TV. I just want to write and tell you that I am a follower of Jesus Christ." Another answer to prayer—sixty years after.

But the most amazing answer came the week after the TV broadcast. When I was five years old, I accepted the Lord Jesus as my Saviour. After that I developed a burden for the people in my town. We lived in Haarlem, quite near the Smedestraat. In this street there were many pubs. Because of the pubs, I often saw many drunken people, some of whom were dragged into the police station on the same street. I wanted so badly to do something to help, but what can a little girl do in such a sad situation? All I could do was pray—and I did a lot of that.

Mother told me later that for a long time every prayer of mine ended with the words, "Lord Jesus, please save those people in the Smedestraat. And save the policemen, too."

Following my TV appearance, I received a letter. "My husband said that it was so nice to hear that you lived in Haarlem. He lived for seventeen years in the Smedestraat, and he worked in the police station in that street. After I heard you on TV, I knew that you would be interested to know that we now know the

Lord personally." It took over seventy years for me to hear that my prayer was answered!

Why do I tell you this? To let you know that no matter how discouraged you may be over your prayers, God never lets you down.

Pray Alone and Together

Prayer is the sturdy answer to worry. I urge you to find a place where you can be alone with the Lord. Let it be your own little private prayer chapel.

I understand that Susanna Wesley, mother of Charles Wesley, had her own little private prayer closet. When things got bad in the Wesley household— the children screaming, money scarce, the roof leaking—she would reach down and grab the hem of her long shirt. Separating it from the many long petticoats women wore in those days, she would pull the outer skirt up over her head and close herself in. There she would meet the Lord and commune with Him, returning to her hectic world refreshed and revived.

Prayer should be informal and to the point: conversations with God, so to speak. Nice words do not count. Be definite. If you have a nervous tummy, do not ask the Lord to take it away. Rather, confess where you got it and ask Him to shut the door on the source of your worry.

Pray specific prayers. God does not give stones for bread. If you ask for specific things, you will receive specific answers. Most of us receive not because we ask not, or if we do ask, we ask amiss.

Go to God the same way you would go to your father or mother. Tell Him about your worries. Tell Him you are a sinner because you are anxious and nervous. Be definite. Prayer opens doors to the power that relieves us from anxiety, for God's power is demonstrated in our weakness.

Remember, prayer is not one-way traffic. If it were, it would be similar to someone coming into your house, asking a question, and then leaving without waiting for an answer. Prayer is both asking and receiving, speaking and listening. Yes, that takes time. But you can learn how to converse with God secretly.

But there is more. Not only do we find help for our anxiety by praying alone, but also when we pray with others and have others pray for us. Jesus says He enjoys joining a small group of even two or three who are praying in his name. ". . . I will be right there among them" (Matthew 18:20). What a marvelous promise! But how many take advantage of it? The best place for group prayer is in the family. Are you a mother? Call the children and ask them to pray with you. Tell them you are anxious and worried, and ask them to join you in prayer.

The devil smiles when we make plans. He laughs when we get too busy. But he trembles when we pray—especially when we pray together. Remember, though, that it is God who answers, and He always answers in a way that He knows is best for everybody.

From My Notebook

Prayer is the signature of the soul on the correspondence with our Creator.

Prayer changes our attention from the problem to the Power, from anxiety to the Almighty.

Is prayer your steering wheel or your spare tire? Keep on top of your circumstances by keeping the morning watch. Don't allow the circumstances to come on top of you.

> We mutter, we sputter—
> We fume and we spurt.
> We mumble and grumble—
> Our feelings get hurt.
>
> We can't understand things—
> Our vision gets dim,
> When all that we need—
> Is a moment with Him.

To pray only when in peril is to use safety belts only in heavy traffic.

> Fear knocked at the door.
> Faith answered
> No one was there.

9

God's Answers to Prayer

His love has no limit, His grace has no measure.
  His power no boundary known unto men;
For out of His infinite riches in Jesus,
  He giveth and giveth and giveth again.

ANNIE JOHNSON FLINT

I know many people who trust the Lord for their
eternal safety, but they have no faith for the cares of
every day. They would find it easy to die, for they
know God has promised them a mansion in heaven. In
fact, some of them would like to die, just to escape this
world. They have no faith for today—just for tomorrow. They do not see that their daily problems are the
material from which God builds His miracles.

Once, when I was a little girl, I remember coming to
my father with a broken doll. He was busy in the
watch shop repairing clocks and watches, but he
stopped what he was doing and took special pains to
fix my ragged old doll's broken arm. Why did he take
this so seriously? Because he saw the doll through the
eyes of his little girl. Your heavenly Father loves you.
He sees your problems through your eyes. He loves us
all and understands our problems. He cares.

When I was in the German concentration camp at Ravensbruck, one bitter winter morning I woke up with a bad cold. My nose was running. Back in Holland I would have been able to adjust to a cold, because I would have a tissue or a hankie to blow my nose. But in the concentration camp, and without a hankie, I felt I could not stand it.

"Well, why don't you pray for a hankie?" Betsie asked.

I started to laugh. There we were, with the world falling apart around us. We were locked in a camp where thousands of people were being executed each week, being beaten to death, or put through unbearable suffering—and Betsie suggests I pray for a hankie! If I were to pray for anything, it would be for something big, not something little, like that.

But before I could object, Betsie began to pray. "Father, in the name of Jesus I now pray for a hankie for Corrie, because she has a bad cold."

I shook my head and walked away. Very shortly after, I was standing by the window when I heard someone call my name. I looked out and spotted a friend of mine, another prisoner, who worked in the hospital.

"Here you are," she said in a matter-of-fact tone. "Take it. I bring you a little present."

I opened the little parcel, and inside was a handkerchief! I could hardly believe my eyes. "How did you know? Did Betsie tell you? Did you know I had a cold?"

She shrugged. "I know nothing. I was busy sewing handkerchiefs out of an old piece of sheet, and there was a voice in my heart saying, 'take a hankie to Corrie ten Boom.' So, there is your gift. From God."

That pocket hankerchief, made from an old piece of

sheet, was a message from heaven for me. It told me that there is a heavenly Father who hears, even if one of His children on this little planet prays for a tiny little thing like a hankie. Not only does He hear, but He speaks to another of His children and says, "Bring a hankie to Corrie ten Boom."

Why should I worry, when I can pray? We are God's children—His own children. Here is an old and well-known story that taught me a deep lesson.

A boy made a little ship. It was a work of art, and he had put many weeks of work into its construction. When it was ready, he took it to the river, and it could really float. He held the rope tightly in his hand, but suddenly a strong wind swept the boat away with such force that the rope broke. The river was deep and wild, and the boy knew that he had lost his ship.

After a few weeks, to his great joy, he saw his ship in the show window of a shop. He went to the shopkeeper and told him that the ship belonged to him, that he had made it. But the man said, "Only the person who gives me the price I am asking for it will have the ship."

The boy went home crying and told his father, who advised him, "I think you must try to make some money and buy the ship."

The boy worked all his spare time until he had enough money and bought his toy from the man. With his ship in his hand, he came home and said, "It's twice mine! I made it, and I bought it."

Can we trust the Lord Jesus, who made us and bought us? We surely can. We are twice His!

A minister in Russia gave me another good illustration. Many people lived in a large apartment house. All the junk was taken to the basement and it was overfull. In a corner stood a harp that was broken, and nobody was able to repair it.

Once a tramp asked if he could spend the night in the house. "There is such a severe snowstorm. May I stay here?"

"We have no room for you, but you could sleep in the basement." They emptied a corner and put some straw on the floor.

After some hours, the owner of the harp suddenly heard music in the basement. She ran downstairs and saw the tramp playing the harp.

"How did you repair my harp? I could not find anybody who was able to do it."

The tramp answered, "When I was young I made this harp, and when you make something, you can repair it."

Who made you? Do you think He can repair you?

The *No* Answer

When Betsie and I were in Ravensbruck, she became very ill. I took her to the prison hospital and she asked me, "Corrie, please pray with me. Ask the Lord Jesus to heal me. He has said, 'If you shall lay hands upon the sick they shall be healed.' Please do that for me."

I prayed and laid hands on her, and both Betsie and I trusted the Lord for healing. The next morning, I ran from the barracks and looked through the window of the hospital and found Betsie's bed was empty. I ran from window to window, until I finally saw her body. They were getting ready to take it to the crematorium. It was the darkest moment of my life.

Then, just a few days later, I was summoned to the

prison office. For some reason, I was being released from prison. Surely it was a clerical error, but whatever the cause, I was free to go. It was a miracle of God.

When I came to the office, I discovered nobody there knew that Betsie was dead. So I asked, "Is my sister also free?"

"No. She stays here until the end of the war."

"Can I stay with her?"

The official became furious and shouted at me. "Disappear! Get out of here!"

Suddenly I saw God's side of what had happened. Suppose Betsie had gotten better and I had to leave her behind? I would have been forced to return to Holland and leave her alone in that horrible camp. I could not have stood it. But she had been released from the concentration camp and was now enjoying all the glory of heaven. I walked out of the camp that day praising and thanking the Lord for that unanswered prayer. Yet it really wasn't unanswered. It was answered in God's way, not mine.

So often we pray and then fret anxiously, waiting for God to hurry up and do something. All the while God is waiting for us to calm down, so He can do something through us.

There is a vast difference between prayer in faith and faith in prayer. Faith in prayer is very common. Prayer in faith is so uncommon that our Lord questions if He will find any of it on earth when He comes back. Prayer in faith is a commanded duty; it is always reverently making known our requests unto God in full confidence that, if we ask anything according to His will, He hears us; and that according to our faith an answer to our prayers will be granted us.

Praying in faith comes from an abiding faith in the Person prayed to—the confidence is in Him. It is based on a knowledge of who He is, and on a trusted conviction that He is worthy to be trusted. Praying in faith is the act of a simple-hearted child of God. Can we teach ourselves to pray in faith? We can indeed train ourselves, but the joyful experience is that it is the Spirit of God who does the job. So give room in your heart for the Holy Spirit.

From My Notebook

Prayer is opening up our sluicegates to the mighty ocean of God.

BISHOP WESTCOTT

Satan trembles when he sees
The weakest saint upon his knees.
The host of hell can that one rout,
Who meets him with a praiseful shout.

The Holy Spirit does not give a clear blueprint of the rest of your life, but only of a moment, one by one.

We can't solve problems for others. We can introduce them to the Lord.

As a camel kneels before his master to have him remove his burden at the end of the day, so kneel each night and let the Master take your burden.

If a care is too small to be turned into a prayer, it is too small to be made into a burden.

Here then is my charge: First, supplications, prayers, intercessions and thanksgivings should be made on behalf of all men . . . .

1 Timothy 2:1 PHILLIPS

Prayer is the same as the breathing of air for the lungs. Exhaling makes us get rid of our dirty air. Inhaling gives clean air. To exhale is to confess, to inhale is to be filled with the Holy Spirit.

10

Trust

You should therefore be most careful, my brothers, that there should not be in any of you that wickedness of heart which refuses to trust, and deserts the cause of the living God.

Hebrews 3:12 PHILLIPS

We continue to share in all that Christ has for us so long as we steadily maintain, until the end, the trust with which we began. God's love for us never changes—of this we must be confident.

We sin, and our sin comes between our souls and God, as a dark cloud comes between the sun and the earth, and our communion with Him is broken. We are unable to live in the enjoyment of God's love for us when sin stands in our way. Our temptation to sin by worrying comes from the evil one, but we must remember that he can only come through an open door. Calling on Jesus' name sends him back, along with any of his brood, because they hate and fear the name of their Conqueror. They get away from the sound of that name as fast as they can.

Our fearless testimony makes the power of the blood of Jesus effective. There is great need for overcomers in this world, and our Lord earnestly calls for men to follow in His steps and in His strength. He won the decisive victory over our enemies, but everyone must make that victory his own on the battlefield of his own life. In Jesus' great name, we can. By His grace, we will.

Our worry is often due to physical causes. Overwork always makes a sensitive spirit worry and hurry, which in turn overworks our nerves, until we see things in a distorted manner. It is a vicious circle, because worry usually makes us keep working harder, until we finally drop from exhaustion—physical and mental. At that point, we go to God for help, but we have already begun to listen to the devil, so we go to God with a sense of inferiority, which is the devil's message!

Some years ago, I had a very difficult problem and did not see the answer. I talked it over with a good friend. We looked at each other, and on both of our faces there was an expression of defeat. Suddenly my friend stood up. She hit the table with her hand and said, "Do we really think that the enormous power that caused Jesus to come out of the grave is not enough for our problem?" Then I saw the smallness of my faith. Yes, the same Spirit that raised Christ from the dead is willing to work in you.

But if we want to be victorious over our fears through Jesus' victory and strength, we must also be obedient. It was Jesus' obedience that defeated the enemy at every turn, until the climax of Calvary was reached.

Confessed Sins

Once we realize that fear, anxiety, and worry are sins, and then confess these sins to God, what happens? The Bible says, "He has removed our sins as far away from us as the east is from the west" (Psalms 103:12). "I've blotted out your sins; they are gone like morning mist at noon! Oh, return to me, for I have paid the price to set you free" (Isaiah 44:22). "But if we confess our sins to him, he can be depended on to forgive us and to cleanse us from every wrong . . ." (1 John 1:9).

Did you ever see a cloud again, after it had disappeared? No, the cloud that appears afterward is a different one. We do not honor God by asking forgiveness a second time for the same sin. Say, "God has beaten this thing. He had forgiven this sin and forgotten it. I can do the same in His strength." Remember that the victory has been won. Claim that victory as your own, and it will be your own in fact. There is far more victory within your reach than you have realized. Reach out your hand and take as your very own what has been done for you. Reckon yourself dead to the sin of worry.

Say with Paul, ". . . I can do everything God asks me to with the help of Christ who gives me the strength and power" (Philippians 4:13). Commit the past to God, and don't be enchained with it again.

As He cleanses our cups, He fills them to overflowing with His Holy Spirit. We must remember that our cups can be kept clean. Everything that the light of God shows as sin, we can confess and carry to the fountain of water of life, and it is gone, both from God's sight and from our hearts.

A little girl broke a beautiful antique cup. Crying, she brought it to her mother. The mother saw that the little one was sorry, and said, "I forgive you. Throw the pieces in the garbage can."

The next day, the little girl saw the pieces in the garbage can. She took them and brought them to her mother again. "I am so sorry, Mother, that I broke your cup yesterday," she cried.

The mother replied, "Leave that in the garbage can, where it belongs. Remember my forgiveness." A confessed sin is dead. Give it a burial.

"Hallelujah!"

Handel's chorus was resounding through the evening air. "Hallelujah! And He shall reign for ever and ever."

I had never heard it sung so perfectly and in such beautiful surroundings.

We were in Japan. The moon and stars were as clear as they can only be in that country. Far away we even saw the white peaks of Mount Fuji.

"Hallelujah! The Lord God omnipotent reigneth."

I had never heard it sung *a capella*, without musical accompaniment. It was as if angels were singing.

I knew the girls. They were the students for whom I had been holding a daily Bible study for the last two weeks, and they were going to the same hall as I, where I was expected to answer questions.

That evening I had to listen most to their worry about sins. I prayed that the Lord would give me a clear answer for them. They were Christian girls, but what a lack of joy they had about the finished work of Jesus at the cross. I asked them a question. "When you rehearsed the 'Hallelujah Chorus,' did you make mistakes?"

The girls giggled. Japanese girls giggle much.

"Many."

"But when you were singing outside in that

Japanese moonlit evening, you did not think of those mistakes, otherwise you might have repeated them. Girls, never wait to confess your sins. The devil accuses us night and day. I will tell you something. Sunday morning I spoke in your church."

"Yes, we remember it. You gave us much, but it was so short."

I thought the same, and your pastor had promised me a long time. I asked him, 'Because I can speak only once in your church, give me as long as possible. Make your preliminaries short.' He promised me, but did not do it. We started the service at 10 o'clock, and at 11 o'clock he was still busy with the *Book of Common Prayer.* That moment the Holy Spirit showed me that I was very impatient. I knew that that was a sin, and at 11 o'clock I brought it to the Lord and asked forgiveness. When we confess our sins, He is faithful and just to forgive us and to cleanse us with His blood. Suddenly I saw that the words of the *Book of Common Prayer* were not just preliminaries, but truths that the Lord uses for His honor.

"Why did I tell you that it was 11 o'clock? Because the devil accuses us before God and our own hearts. It is possible that he said to God at 11:05, 'Do You see Corrie ten Boom in Your church and how impatient she is?' I believe that God answered him, 'I already know it. Five minutes ago Corrie told me. It is forgiven and cleansed.'

"Girls, be sure that you are always five minutes earlier than the accuser. Then you lose your worry about your sins. The reason Jesus came to earth was to save sinners. He died for you, so that you could be forgiven, and He lives for you and in you by His Holy Spirit, to make you overcomers. When you worry about your sins it is because you know them through the accuser who has told you, 'That sin is typically you. That is your nature, and you will remain like that your whole life. There is no hope for you.'

"The devil, the accuser, is a liar. When the Holy Spirit convicts you of sin, it is always in the floodlight of the finished work of Jesus at the cross. He tells you: 'Exactly for these sins Jesus died. Confess and be cleansed.'

"Do you remember what I taught you this week—what the Bible says about repented sins? 'As far as the east is from the west, so far does he remove our transgressions from us' [*see* Psalms 103]. He throws them into the depths of the sea, forgiven and forgotten, and to warn the accuser, He puts a sign saying No Fishing Allowed. Girls, instead of worrying about your sins, sing again, 'Hallelujah! King of kings and Lord of lords.' "

It sounded even more beautiful than when I had heard it outside, but this time I saw the happy faces, some still wet with tears.

The Word of God

God's promises were never meant to be thrown aside as waste paper. He intended that they should be used. God's gold is not miser's money, but is minted to be traded with. Nothing pleases our Lord better than to see His promises put into circulation; He loves to see His children bring them up to Him, and say, "Lord, do as You have said."

Charles H. Spurgeon

We deny the work of Jesus Christ and stand power-less before the enemy if we doubt the integrity of the Word of God. The bank account of the Bible is not frozen.

Someone told me, "In the Bible there are 17,000 promises." I don't know if that is true, but even if there were only 17, the quality is so great that the quantity is not too important.

> . . . He has given you the whole world to use, and life and even death are your servants. He has given you all of the present and all of the future. All are yours, and you belong to Christ, and Christ is God's.
>
> 1 Corinthians 3:22, 23

When you check your inventory of blessings from God, it shows you have received good measure, pressed down and running over. Do not say, "I am too great a sinner to appropriate God's promises. Perhaps good Christians may do that, but not I." God always hears a prayer of faith. Put all your needs on the table and then say thank You.

Once a factory owner had a very expensive, compli-cated machine that he needed for his work. It broke down, and there was nobody who could repair it. The owner sent a telegram to the machine factory: "Send an expert." The very next day, an unimpressive man arrived at the airport. The owner sent another tele-gram to protest that the man they had sent was unsatis-factory. He wore old clothing, he seemed very uneducated—the owner was not at all happy with him. The answer that came back from the machine factory was, "That man is the designer of your machine."

Don't you think our own Creator can find the answers to our problems? Jesus is able to untangle all the snarls in your soul, to banish all complexes, and to transform even your fixed habit patterns. All you must do is trust Him.

From My Notebook

A dying old man said, "I am too sick to remember one promise of God. But I don't worry, because God does not forget them."

If the enemy cannot keep you from working, then he comes up behind you and pushes you and tries to kill you with overwork.

When the devil can't make you bad, he makes you busy.

Elijah was so sure of God that he added difficulties by throwing water over the altar. We, in our unbelief, try to help God.

In the forest fire, there is always one place where the fire cannot reach. It is the place where the fire has already burned itself out. Calvary is the place where the fire of God's judgment against sin burned itself out completely. It is there that we are safe.

The strength we claim from God's Word does not depend on circumstances. Circumstances will be difficult, but our strength will be sufficient.

Your strength, my weakness—here they always
  meet,
When I lay down my burden at Your feet;
The things that seem to crush will in the end
Be seen as rungs, on which I did ascend!

Not one sparrow (What do they cost? Two for a penny?) can fall to the ground without your Father knowing it. And the very hairs of your head are all numbered. So don't worry! You are more valuable to him than many sparrows.

Matthew 10:29–31

If you make a compromise with surrender, you can remain interested in the abundant life, all the riches of freedom, love, and peace, but it is the same as looking at a display in a shop window. You look through the window but do not go in and buy. You will not pay the price—Surrender.

E. STANLEY JONES

11

Surrender

Jesus told him, "If you want to be perfect, go and sell everything you have and give the money to the poor, and you will have treasure in heaven; and come, follow me." But when the young man heard this, he went away sadly, for he was very rich.

Matthew 19:21, 22

That rich young ruler gladly kept all the commandments, and he searched out even more ways to serve his God. But when Jesus told him he would have to give up everything he treasured in his life, the young man simply could not do it.

J. H. Jowett comments on this:

He hallowed the inch, but not the mile. He would go part of the way, but not to the end. And the peril is upon us all. We give ourselves to the Lord, but we reserve some liberties. We offer Him our home, but we mark some rooms "Private." And that word, "Private," denying the Lord admission, crucifies Him afresh.

My being a tramp for the Lord, going over the whole world, was real training for me in surrender and trust. I learned that the safest place in the world is in the center of the will of God. This is always true, even sometimes when it seems as if following God's will is physically dangerous.

Shortly after the war, I was alone in America. It was Saturday morning in Chicago. I paid the taxi driver and stepped into the YWCA. The lady in the office did not look very happy to see me.

"The office is almost closed, lady," she said.

"Have you a room for me?" I asked.

"No. Come back on Monday."

"Will you telephone the nearest police station, then, and ask them if I can sleep in a cell tonight?"

She looked very surprised. "Why?"

"Well, I come from Holland, and in Holland no woman has to stay in the street during the night. There is always room in a police station, in a cell, and I am sure that in America it will be the same. I would not think of remaining on the street all night in a town like Chicago."

She left the office for a minute, then came back and said, "We have found a room for you."

That was exactly what I had hoped would happen, and I went to my room. It was not the most beautiful room. It was very high up in the building and very small, but much more luxurious than the cell I was living in a year before, in the prison camp.

I did not go out on Sunday. It was raining, and I had discovered that when it rains in America, it pours. I needed some time for rest and for talking with the Lord. As a matter of fact, my first experience in Chicago had scared me. I did not know anyone there, and it was such a big, strange city to face alone.

That Sunday in my room, I had a good talk with the Lord. I confessed my fears to Him and surrendered the whole trip through America to His will. Two weeks after, the Lord blessed my ministry in America in a way that must have made the angels rejoice. The Lord did much good work through the many talks in all the little churches. God opened the doors and the hearts of Chicago for me, and Moody Bible Institute gave me such a welcome that I have never since felt alone in Chicago.

My Lord knows the way through the wilderness—all I have to do is follow and to put my hand into His hand. He holds me.

There is only one force more powerful than fear, and that is faith. Does your need seem big to you? Then make sure that God knows how big it looks to your eyes, and He will treat it as such. He will never belittle it, however trivial. He will not laugh at it, or at us. He never forgets how large our problems look to us.

Does your need seem as big as the throne of grace? Do we not there—and there alone—see it in the right proportion?

We ask, "Do you believe that the Lord is your Shepherd?"

"Yes, but . . . ."

That fatal word *but* shows that we do not believe the Lord is our Shepherd. "Yes, I believe it, *but* I do not have victory over my bad temper, and I am not able to win souls. I worry over things. I do not have peace and joy."

The testimony of victory puts *but* into the right place. "I am passing through a time of great sorrow and trouble, *but* the Lord is my Shepherd. I have been discouraged about my past accomplishment, *but* the Lord is my Shepherd."

Set yourself against being disturbed by disturbing things. Say to yourself, "Being upset is useless. It has bad results, it is sinful. It reproaches my Master. I will not be upset."

Amy Carmichael wrote:

> He, Who loved you unto death, is speaking to you. Listen, do not be deaf and blind to Him. And as you keep quiet and listen, you will know, deep down in your heart, that you are loved. As the air is around about you, so is His love around about you now. Trust that love to guide your lives. It will never, never fail. You know how we have watched the great sea washing over the rocks, flooding them till they overflow? That is what the love of God does for us. We have no love in ourselves and our pools would soon be empty if it were not for that glorious inexhaustible sea of love which extends to you and me. Lord, do Thou turn me all into love, and all my love into obedience, and let my obedience be without interruption.

If His will be your will, and His way be your way, then all your insufficiency and inaptitude shall be met by the sufficiency of His grace.

Obey the voice of the Lord Jesus, who says, "Come unto me, all ye that labour and are heavy laden, and I will give you rest" (Matthew 11:28 KJV). Come! Like a mother says to a fearful child, "Come." Nothing else is necessary. When you come to Him, He does the job.

Jesus says, "Behold, I stand at the door, and knock: if any man hear my voice, and open the door, I will come in . . ." (Revelation 3:20 KJV).

"But as many as received him, to them gave he power to become the sons of God . . ." (John 1:12 KJV). That means to become a member of the very family of God, and ". . . Except a man be born again, he cannot see the kingdom of God" (John 3:3 KJV). We cannot expect peace or rest until we personally find it in Jesus Christ. When we do, we can say, ". . . For I know whom I have believed, and am persuaded that he is able to keep that which I have committed unto him against that day" (2 Timothy 1:12 KJV).

Know that Christ is the Lord of all: your mind, your spirit, your body. Let Christ's teachings live in your heart, making you rich in true wisdom. Put everything in His hands.

The first time a cowboy heard the story of Jesus riding on an unbroken colt, he exclaimed, "What wonderful hands He must have had!" Consider the hands of Christ: artist's hands that created all the beauty of this world; love-pierced hands of the kindest Friend that man ever had; hands that are aching to take our own and guide us in ways that are good for us; skillful hands, worthy of our trust and love.

Let us let Him clasp our hands a little tighter, and trust Him a little more than ever before—that our paths may be straighter and gladder than in the past. Let us make more time for prayer, so that we increase the pressure of that hand on ours. Their touch is so light, and the whisper so soft, it is easy to miss them.

A young, discouraged artist fell asleep beside the picture that he was trying to complete. His master quietly entered the room, and, bending over the sleeping pupil, placed on the canvas, with his own skillful hand, the beauty that the painting lacked.

When we, tired and spent, lay down the work done

in our own strength, our own great Master will make perfect our picture. He will remove every stain, every blemish, and every failure from our service. He will add the brightest luster to our service, and He will give us the highest honor for our work.

Shall we not surrender to the One who can make us His victorious artists? Paul wrote:

> My brothers, I do not consider myself to have grasped it fully even now. But I do concentrate on this: I forget all that lies behind me and with hands outstretched to whatever lies ahead I go straight for the goal—my reward the honour of my high calling by God in Christ Jesus.
>
> Philippians 3:13, 14 PHILLIPS

> Now to Him who is able to keep you from falling and to present you before his glory without fault and with unspeakable joy, to the only God, our saviour, be glory and majesty, power and authority . . . .
>
> Jude 24 PHILLIPS

You may write to Corrie ten Boom at Box 2040, Orange, CA 92669. Her magazine *The Hiding Place* is published bimonthly from the same address.